DATE DUE

HIGHSMITH   #LO-45228

RACE CAR LEGENDS

CHELSEA HOUSE PUBLISHERS

RACE CAR LEGENDS

THE
JARRETTS

Richard Huff

CHELSEA HOUSE PUBLISHERS
Philadelphia

Frontis: Three generations of racers: Jason (left), Ned (center), and Dale Jarrett.

Produced by Type Shoppe II Productions, Ltd.
Chestertown, Maryland

Picture research by Joseph W. Wagner

CHELSEA HOUSE PUBLISHERS

Editor in Chief: Stephen Reginald
Managing Editor: James Gallagher
Production Manager: Pamela Loos
Art Director: Sara Davis
Picture Editor: Judy L. Hasday
Senior Production Editor: Lisa Chippendale
Publishing Coordinator: James McAvoy
Cover Illustration: Keith Trego

Cover Photos: AP/Wide World Photos

5 7 9 8 6 4

The Chelsea House Publishers World Wide Web site address is
http://www.chelseahouse.com

Library of Congress Cataloging-in-Publication Data
Huff, Richard M.
     The Jarretts / Richard Huff.
        p.   cm. — (Race car legends)
     Includes bibliographical references and index.
     Summary: Discusses the personal lives and racing careers of
the three generations of Jarretts involved in NASCAR racing.
     ISBN 0-7910-5018-1 (alk. paper)
     1. Jarrett, Ned, 1932- —Juvenile literature. 2. Jarrett,
Glenn, 1950- —Juvenile literature. 3. Jarret, Dale, 1956- —
Juvenile literature. 4. Jarrett, Jason, 1975- —Juvenile
literature. 5. Automobile racing drivers—United States—
Biography—Juvenile literature. 6. Stock car racing—United
States—Juvenile literature. [1. Jarrett, Ned, 1932- . 2.
Jarrett, Glenn, 1950- . 3. Jarrett, Dale, 1956- . 4. Jarrett,
Jason, 1975- . 5. Automobile racing drivers. 6. Stock car
racing.] I. Title. II. Series.
GV1032.A1H846 1998
796.72'092'273—dc21
[B]   98-19231
                                                       CIP
                                                       AC

CONTENTS

FATHER AND SON AT DAYTONA

As the laps wore down in the 1993 Daytona 500, superstar driver and then five-time series champion Dale Earnhardt was leading a line of cars in the historic race that included rookie Jeff Gordon, Dale Jarrett, Geoff Bodine, and Hut Stricklin.

With three circuits around the 2.5-mile-long Daytona International Speedway remaining, Jarrett, the son of two-time NASCAR champion Ned Jarrett, stormed past Gordon and was side-by-side with "The Intimidator" Earnhardt, best known for his dominating, aggressive driving style.

Bodine guided his Ford Thunderbird behind Jarrett's Chevy, creating a two-car draft. Gordon then eased his Chevrolet Lumina on the bumper of Earnhardt's car, to form a pack of four cars, side-by-side, out front together running at speeds of nearly 200 miles per hour.

Dale Jarrett lets out a victory yell as he gets out of his car after winning the Daytona 500 in 1993, at the Daytona International Speedway.

In stock car racing, two cars running nose to tail can run faster than one car can alone because of the way they cut through the wind. Now, with less than a lap remaining in the Great American Race—the sport's equivalent of the Super Bowl—four cars were in a position to win the coveted trophy.

The cars of Jarrett and Earnhardt touched momentarily, although the skilled drivers averted a full-scale collision. The draft created by Jarrett and Bodine, however, proved too much for Earnhardt and Gordon. Pushed by Bodine, Jarrett pulled out ahead going into the final corner.

A sellout crowd watches as Kyle Petty and Dale Jarrett lead the rest of the cars at the start of the 35th annual Daytona 500 in 1993.

In the broadcast booth, high above the speedway, Dale's father, Ned, now a member of CBS' on-air team, got an instruction from the broadcast's producer, Bob Stenner. During all live broadcasts, producers talk to their on-air people through small devices in the broadcaster's ear. Normally, the conversations are about upcoming commercials, instant replays, or what the broadcaster should say about a certain driver's on-track position.

But this time the instructions were different. Through his earpiece, Jarrett heard Stenner say, "Ned, root your son home." Jarrett, who had silently been working out his son's strategy, was now free to say what he was thinking.

Jarrett's broadcast-booth colleagues went silent. CBS turned cameras on both Jarretts, the father in the broadcast booth and the son on the track.

"Come on, Dale! Go baby, go!" Ned Jarrett shouted, rising to his feet and shaking his fists in the air. "He's going to make it! Dale Jarrett's going to win the Daytona 500!"

Dale Jarrett held onto the lead and beat Earnhardt across the finish line by .19 seconds, less than two car lengths.

For even casual fans of sport, it is well known that the broadcaster should never be part of the story. For a reporter or commentator, cheering for any of the participants is a major "no-no." Broadcasters must remain objective and impartial at all times. And for Jarrett, who during his racing career became known as "Gentleman Ned" for his calm on- and off-track demeanor, this sort of outburst was highly unusual.

"I'm not the real emotional type. I'm not Dick Vitale," Ned said, referring to the usually loud basketball announcer. "But this was something different. It's the greatest feeling I can have, the greatest feeling I've ever had, no doubt," he continued. "Any accomplishment that I had winning any of my races or those two championships do not mean nearly as much as this does."

Television sports critics, who in any other case would lambaste a broadcaster for rooting for a player, embraced Jarrett's CBS performance as something to be cherished. It was a sports moment that would be hard to match.

"Stenner asked the others to back off and told me to do the call, he said, 'Be a father.' That got me pumped up. I got a little more emotional. It was a natural father's reaction, I think," Jarrett explained.

But it was much more. In a way, Dale Jarrett's win in stock car racing's most prestigious event brought full circle a racing journey started by Ned Jarrett back in the '50s, when he debuted as a local driver in North Carolina. That trek brought Ned Jarrett fame, fortune, and a child who had now won the Daytona 500. He had earned two championships and 50 career wins, but Ned Jarrett had never won the Daytona 500.

After emerging from his car, Dale spoke to his father on a two-way radio: "You came so close when you ran out of gas in '63," he told his dad. "I got this one for you and all the family."

The win was only the second in Dale Jarrett's career, and the first for car owner Joe Gibbs, who in a previous career won three Super Bowls as coach of the Washington Redskins.

"I had three things going for me," Dale said. "I had a good car, good luck, and God on my

side. . . . That's what it takes to win the Daytona 500."

Although his father retired when he was just a kid, Dale Jarrett had been around racing, or at least influenced by the sport in some way, just about all of his life. After leaving the sport

Washington Redskins coach Joe Gibbs, left, owner of the Interstate Batteries Chevrolet that Dale Jarrett drove to a win at the Daytona 500 in 1993.

in 1965, Ned Jarrett remained a racing broadcaster and track promoter in North Carolina. Dale's older brother, Glenn, had also raced for a while, although he eventually turned to broadcasting full time.

"I sat in my dad and mom's car when I was eight and nine years old, pretending I was driving in the Daytona 500," Dale said. "Of course, I won every time back then. Now, I really have won it."

The win was significant for Dale because he had now proven he could make it in the sport in which his father had made such a mark three decades earlier. Despite attempts by his

Dale Jarrett, from Hickory, North Carolina, takes the checkered flag to win the 1993, 35th Daytona 500. Behind Jarrett is Dale Earnhardt, second, and Geoff Bodine, third.

parents to steer him away from racing—he was a multisport star and they hoped he would pursue professional golf full time— Dale had overcome some lean years to now be included among an elite bunch of drivers. "I've gone back and watched the replay of my father's call three times," Dale said a few weeks later. "For a few minutes, the Jarretts took over national television. It's a day I'll never forget."

Neither will Ned. He was as proud as a peacock over his son's accomplishment. "You never know how your kids are going to turn out, so you try to set examples and help them along the way," Ned once told a reporter. "We've been extremely fortunate that ours have turned out so well. We've been blessed in that sense."

THE
EARLY DAYS

Ned Jarrett was born on October 12, 1932, in Newton, North Carolina, a small town northwest of Charlotte.

At the time, Herbert Hoover was president of the United States and the formation of the National Association for Stock Car Auto Racing (NASCAR) was still 16 years away.

Like most kids in Newton, Jarrett grew up on a farm. His father, Homer, ran the family-owned sawmill which turned raw trees into usable lumber for the rapidly growing region.

Stock car racing was also in its infancy. There was no formal organization to oversee the sport as there is today. What loosely organized races existed were predominantly in the south. And in fact, stock car racing's roots are directly tied to the trends and laws of the time in the United States.

Ned Jarrett was born a year before the United States lifted the ban on the manufac-

This Prohibition-era rum-running automobile was equipped with an apparatus for throwing out a smoke screen. It was captured after a thrilling chase for two miles through the streets of Washington, D.C.

ture, transportation, and consumption of alcohol. From 1920 to 1933, the government banned the sale of alcoholic drinks, such as beer, wine, and liquor. Despite the legal ramifications, the lure of tax-free money, combined with public demand, led many people to make alcohol in underground operations.

People who manufactured illegal liquor were called "moonshiners," and the equipment they used to produce the alcoholic beverages were called "stills." To get their product from the stills, located in the woods throughout the south, moonshiners hired drivers who would use cars to move the liquor to the buyers.

These "runners" souped up their cars by stripping them of any unnecessary interior weight—seats were removed to make room for the bottles of alcohol—and the engines were finely tuned. In addition, they tried to make their cars faster than those of the police, just in case they got caught driving down a road with a carload of the illegal product.

When they weren't hauling liquor, moonshine runners often raced against each other. It is not surprising that two men, standing around talking about how fast their cars were, would eventually race against each other to prove who was really the fastest. These incidents led to organized races, which were often held in open fields. When people realized that fans would pay to see the races, organized stock car racing was born.

Ned's parents got him interested in racing as a kid. His father, however, was not overjoyed with the sport's image. In addition to the moonshining, the sport was hurt by shady promoters who often ran off with the prize money before the race was over, leaving the participants empty-handed. And because it was run on dirt tracks, the drivers, the fans, and everyone else usually left the race covered with dust.

But despite his father's concerns, Ned was bitten by the racing bug. And the sport of racing moved to improve its image in 1948, when William Henry Getty France and a group of race promoters from around the country formed NASCAR. The organization's mission

Typical scene of early dirt track stock car racing using standard vehicles and no safety devices.

was to improve conditions for the fans, clean up the sport overall, and provide a national umbrella, or sanctioning body, to oversee all aspects of the sport.

Five years later, when he was 21, Ned Jarrett hooked up with another local race fan named John Lentz. Together they worked on a race car, which was basically a beefed-up street vehicle.

In the early days of racing, the cars were stock, which meant that the cars used in racing had to be those available at the typical car dealer's showroom.

The technology then was nowhere near as advanced as it is today. There were no seat belts, no roll bars, and no racing slicks. Most racers drove their cars to the track and removed the headlights and taillights before the race. If they didn't wreck the car, when the race was over they would replace the missing parts and drive the cars home.

With Lentz driving and Jarrett working on the car, the team made its debut in 1953 at the brand new Hickory Motor Speedway, in Hickory, North Carolina. Ned's father was still adamant that his son not get mixed up in racing, and Ned was just as adamant that he would race.

"I just simply didn't discuss it," Ned said. "I didn't think that much about it and I didn't think it would make that much difference."

They decided finally that Ned could be a partner in the car as long as he did not drive.

But on the night they were to race, Lentz got sick. The other members of the team didn't look any farther than Jarrett as a replacement. He and Lentz had the same build, and with a helmet on, few could tell it wasn't Lentz behind the wheel.

He entered the race as Lentz and finished 10th in the 50-lap event.

"I thought I was in good physical condition, having grown up on a farm, but I was so tired afterward that I had to be helped out of my car," Jarrett said. "Later, I learned the mental strain had really worn me out. Once I learned to relax, I didn't get so tired."

His tiredness notwithstanding, Jarrett fell in love with driving, even though it was with another man's name. Jarrett kept racing under his assumed name, but found it was hard to keep his identity secret.

He ran under Lentz's name nearly a dozen times before he got his first win. And, because he wasn't supposed to be driving, the victory celebration was subdued. "Finally, I lucked out and won," Jarrett said. "And living in a small community, it got back to him."

Having seen his earlier warnings go unheeded, Homer Jarrett gave his blessing for his son to continue racing, but this time under his own name.

With this encouragement from his father, Ned Jarrett's racing career officially began. At the same time, the building blocks of NASCAR were coming together.

3

NED JARRETT'S RACING CAREER

Ned Jarrett's success at the Hickory Motor Speedway instilled in him a sense of great confidence. Though never a hard charger, Jarrett's smooth and steady style made him a consistent performer on the track. Off the track, he was known as an all-around good guy.

In 1953, armed with this new-found confidence, Jarrett decided he wanted to race with the men now competing on NASCAR's Grand National series, which was the forerunner of the current Winston Cup series. Married and with a three-year-old son, Glenn, Jarrett ventured into the big leagues of stock car racing.

He made his first Grand National start on August 29, 1953, in a 100-mile race held at the Hickory Motor Speedway. He finished 11th in a field of 12 cars. He next set his sights on a larger facility: the newly created Darlington Speedway in South Carolina. The track was

Ned Jarrett gets hugs from his wife, right, and Vicki Johnson, Miss Southern 500, after he won the Southern 500 Stock Car Race at the Darlington Speedway.

built in 1950 by developer Harold Brasington as the first super speedway on what was then NASCAR's Grand National circuit.

Darlington, originally built at 1.25 miles in length and later expanded to 1.375 miles long, was the fastest track on the circuit. Its egg-shaped design was difficult for drivers to manage. The buzz that developed around the facility later dubbed "Too Tough to Tame" proved too tough for Jarrett to resist. "I thought I was good enough to do that," he said.

Ned continued racing primarily in NASCAR's sportsman division, which is the equivalent of today's Busch Grand National division. At the same time, he dabbled a bit in the Grand National series, picking up a race or two each year. Although selective on the top level, Jarrett dominated in the sportsman division. He won the NASCAR Sportsman Championship in 1957 and again in 1958.

Just as Jarrett was growing as a driver, so too was NASCAR racing. The cars, still relatively stock, were becoming more sophisticated. There were no giant changes but instead a gradual evolution as drivers became more inventive. The minor changes included beefing up the suspension, taking out the rear passenger seats, adding primitive roll bar setups, and most important, adding crude seatbelt setups.

Having mastered the short-track circuit, Jarrett graduated to the Grand National circuit full time in 1959.

His off-track demeanor, combined with his on-track style, earned him the nickname "Gentleman Ned" from his competitors. His conservative driving style came out of necessity, he said. He didn't have a lot of money, so if he crashed, his racing career would end suddenly. "You either had to run up front and be dramatic, and if you broke down, okay, or be conservative," he said. "To do that, you had to take care of the equipment back then. Some people labeled you a conservative driver. I learned pretty quickly in the sport that you had to finish before you could win. I learned how to handle a car to make it last. That was the concept I chose."

By then, off the track, Jarrett's family life was in full swing. Son Dale was born in 1956, and daughter Patti on August 31, 1959.

On the track, however, Jarrett's time away from home and the time dedicated to his sport was increasing rapidly.

In 1959, his first full season on the Grand National series, Jarrett started 17 events, picking up two wins and earning $3,860 in prize money. A year later, he started 40 events, won five races, and increased his earnings to $25,438.

He improved his performance using the steady style he developed early in his career. He also was able to boost his overall points totals by performing extremely well on short tracks, which at the time still played host to a majority of the events. "I was not, and am not, a speed demon," Jarrett told writer Kim Chapin in the book *Fast As White Lightning*. "I liked competition, but I wanted the car to feel comfortable . . . if it didn't, I'd slow it down enough to where it did. I didn't try to be a hero. I knew for a fact that there were plenty of people who were as physically capable as I, and maybe some more so, of turning that steering wheel and getting around the track."

Jarrett said his strength on the track was looking ahead further than other drivers, which helped him anticipate, and often avoid, potential wrecks or other disasters. He had the lowest level of accidents among the drivers of his time.

His consistency paid off in 1961 when he started 46 of NASCAR's 52 races. Although he won just one race, his string of 33 top-10 finishes was enough to put him ahead of Rex White to win the series championship. For his

Ned Jarrett and son Dale, 5, and daughter Patti, 3, go over Jarrett's scrapbook. Jarrett is considered the "Gentleman" of stock car drivers of the NASCAR super speedways.

efforts, Ned Jarrett earned a total of $41,056 for the entire year.

Despite the glory that comes with a championship, an incident off the track changed Jarrett's life forever.

Following his championship, members of the Elk's Club in Newton asked him to take part in their Sunday afternoon induction ceremony for incoming officers. Jarrett saw the event as a chance to prove to local leaders that race car drivers were not bad people.

He prepared for the meeting much the way he'd prepare for a race. He memorized his short speech and practiced it for days. But when he appeared before the group, he could not remember a word. "I was scared to death and it was so embarrassing," he told a reporter. "I made up my mind at that very moment that I'd do whatever it took to make myself a better person."

The next day he attended a meeting for the famed Dale Carnegie public speaking course. He continued with the program for several months until he felt comfortable speaking in front of groups of people.

Following completion of the course, Jarrett, often accompanied by his sons, set out to discuss motorsports with church groups in the south. He turned that one horrible moment in Newton into a positive result, and in the process set an example for his sons of how to deal with people. "I was 11 when Dad saw the light, so to speak," Glenn said. "I remember one night we drove to a Baptist church 50 or 60 miles from home, just so he could speak. There was no pay for it. He did it to make himself better."

4

A CAREER HIGH

In the 1960s, NASCAR underwent several dramatic changes that impacted the sport both on and off the track.

In 1962, Chrysler and the Ford Motor Co., both of whom had pulled out of racing in the late '50s, returned to the sport and provided financial assistance to selected teams. The involvement of these manufacturers was driven by the total dominance of the Chevrolet and Pontiac teams, which had won 18 of the first 20 races of the season. Only Richard Petty, who drove his Plymouth to victory twice, was able to defeat the Chevy and Pontiac teams. Jarrett drove a Chevrolet for Bee Gee Holloway in 1961, but a few seasons later he was driving a Ford for Bondy Long.

In some ways the direct involvement in the sport by the automakers had a positive effect, while in other areas, it did not. Because the

Dale Jarrett (88), following in his father's footsteps, is on his way to crossing the finish line at the Pocono International Raceway, where he won the Pennsylvania 500 NASCAR Race.

car makers demanded wins, drivers were forced to push harder on the track than they may have wanted. And unlike today's sleek racers, the cars of the early '60s did not run as smoothly.

This pressure to win was tough on the drivers. If they didn't win, team owners, pushed by the manufacturers, changed drivers as a means of finding on-track magic. "I don't think the average fan would realize the amount of pressure that was involved," Jarrett said. "There was always somebody that was trying to get your job, and certainly you were aware of it, but it was never anything that really bothered me to the point that I lost sleep over it. If I lost the job, well, fine. I was out there doing my best and that's all I figured anyone could expect."

Jarrett's best was better than most. In 1962, he raced in 52 events and won six times to earn $43,444 in prize money. He finished third in the points standings. In 1963, he drove in 53 races, won eight, and took home $45,844 in prize money to finish fourth overall. And in 1964, he logged 59 races, 15 wins, $71,925 in earnings, and finished second in the points standings.

To the general public, the sport was known for the super speedways such as Daytona, Darlington, and Talladega, the staples of the circuit. The sport was moving away from running on dirt tracks—where it all started—to the asphalt ovals.

Speeds were increasing and safety was still not a major factor in the sport. Drivers didn't wear firesuits as they do today. Most wore street pants, short-sleeved shirts, shoes, and

open-faced helmets. In the late '50s and early '60s, drivers dipped their clothes in a fire-resistant solution that, while able to prevent injury, made the clothes uncomfortable. As a result, many drivers stopped using the liquid.

Seatbelts were just lap belts, similar to the ones that came with the cars. And many cars still had bench seats. 1964 was a particularly

Dale Jarrett drives his Winston Cup car, typical of today's sleek racers, through turn one at the Indianapolis Motor Speedway, qualifying at an average speed of 177.49 mph.

gruesome year for racing: a handful of well-known racers were killed.

The growing danger, and not being with his family as much as he liked, started to wear on Jarrett. NASCAR's schedule was hectic, and the stress and strain of keeping a job were tough. And unlike drivers of today, NASCAR's stars were not millionnaires. What Jarrett earned in all of 1964 could be earned in a single race by a driver in the '90s.

Jarrett started the 1965 season in fine form. By mid-season, he and fellow Ford driver Dick Hutcherson were ahead of all the others for the series championship. But his season was up-ended just 60 laps into a race at Greenville-Pickens Speedway in South Carolina. Jarrett's car died while leading the race. Despite his efforts to pull off the track, he was rammed by another car, which sent him back into traffic. His car was pummeled by others, tearing the car apart with such force that his seat was pulled from its anchors. Jarrett suffered a serious back injury, which doctors told him would take three weeks of hospital rest and then three more months of rehabilitation. That wasn't good enough for Jarrett. He had a race to run the following Thursday night. Jarrett doubled the therapy. With the help of a plastic brace, he raced five days later. He used the brace for three months, and despite serious pain, maintained his lock on the NASCAR points lead.

His one championship notwithstanding, Jarrett longed for a win in the prestigious Southern 500 at Darlington. He felt that if he could win that race his career would be complete. The night before the race, Ned spoke to a Methodist Youth Fellowship group and

asked the kids for their prayers. Their response gave him a sense of confidence going in: "Not that I or any other particular driver might win it," Jarrett said then, "but I went away from there with a genuine feeling that those kids were behind me, that they would say a prayer for me. It made me feel good."

Winning the race wouldn't be easy. Although Jarrett still had the points lead, Hutcherson was strong. Jarrett figured if he was to win the Southern 500, Hutcherson's car would have to falter. As luck would have it, Hutcherson did encounter mechanical troubles after less than

Present day racers face the same dangers as early drivers, but at speeds close to 200 mph. Five drivers crash in the fourth turn at the North Carolina Motor Speedway during the AC-Delco 400 in 1995. Dale Jarrett is in car 28, the Texaco Halvoline Ford.

100 miles, but Jarrett was still far from victory. He, too, suffered from mechanical problems as his Ford began to overheat.

Jarrett dodged several accidents that day, and one by one, his chief competitors started to fall. With 100 miles to go, Darel Dieringer and Fred Lorenzen dropped out of the race, leaving Jarrett in front for the final 63 laps.

Because of his overheating engine, Jarrett had to slow his car from an average of 134 mph to 125 mph. "I was saying a prayer every lap for the last several laps," Jarrett said after the race. "I wasn't the fastest on the track, but I was hoping those fellows who were lapping me would wear themselves out. That's what happened."

His win in front of some 60,000 cheering fans remains his most memorable. "It was the oldest and most prestigious at the time," Jarrett told *Winston Cup Scene.* "It was also a tough track, and the win gave me a great sense of accomplishment. It was also a real highlight for me because I won it by 14 laps— which is still a record."

Dale, who was just nine years old at the time, vividly recalled the day. "That was a pretty special day for all of us," he said. "I remember sitting in the family grandstand in the fourth turn and watching the race and after the race we got to meet Doc and Festus from Gunsmoke in Victory Lane. That was the highlight of the race for me. I knew it was a big race back then because about 80 per cent of Camden, South Carolina was at our house."

The Labor Day weekend win propelled Jarrett to his second NASCAR Grand National Championship. He won 13 of the 54 races he entered and took home $93,625. That season he ran a career-high 13,525 laps, representing a total of 9,121 miles.

Winning the title brought Jarrett to a career crossroads. He had met all of the goals he'd set for himself. He had watched friends die in the sport he loved. And he missed his kids and his wife.

Jarrett was determined to retire. "I'd set goals for myself and vowed that I'd quit when I got there," he said. "I didn't want [the fans] to remember me as a has been. I wanted them to remember me for what I was, the reigning champion."

Midway through the 1965 season, while still the reigning champion, he stepped down at the age of 35. During his career, Ned Jarrett had run in 352 races, won 50, and earned $348,967 in prize money.

FOLLOWING
A TRADITION

Ned Jarrett left the competitive side of racing, but he never left the sport.

His two championships left a legacy that continues today. And even though his sons, Glenn and Dale, were relatively young when he retired, Ned's racing experience left an indelible impression on both of them.

When he retired, Ned returned home and, with a partner, started a consulting business that helped people find franchise businesses. Jarrett paid a fee to have control of a local territory, and informed interested customers about a host of franchise businesses. "I fell in love with the concept," he said. "Unfortunately, the parent company did not perform. I saw what was happening and I got out after a year."

Jarrett never considered taking over his family's lumber business. It simply didn't in-

Driver Dale Jarrett sits in his car as crew members work on the engine in preparation for the AC-Delco 400 NASCAR race. Safety regulations now require helmets, seatbelts, and roll bars.

Driver Dick Trickle, front, leads Dale Jarrett, Randy Lajoie, and Jeff Burton during early laps of the Red Dog 300 at the Charlotte Motor Speedway, Concord, North Carolina in May 1996.

terest him. Instead, he focused on enhancing his public speaking career. And in 1966, Jarrett became a financial partner and promoter for the Hickory Motor Speedway where he started his racing career in 1953. As promoter, he was responsible for staging races and making sure the facility ran properly.

Despite the career he had made for himself in the sport, Jarrett and his wife, Martha, tried to steer their sons away from racing. That was tough to do, however, because during his career, Ned and Martha had usually taken the kids to the track. In addition, the boys had fond memories of their time at the track when their father was racing. When Ned retired, Glenn was 15 and Dale 9. "I have a lot of memories, certainly, growing up around the sport," Dale said. "We didn't get to all of [the races], but a lot of fond memories of going to the races and being in the infield with the other families . . ."

While their fathers were racing, the kids played in the infield. Adding to the fun was the fact that they knew that at least one of them would go to Victory Lane because their dad had been successful on the track.

Both Jarrett boys excelled in school and in sports. Ned and Martha had seen what life on the stock car racing road could do to a family, and they were still unsure, even in the '70s, whether it was possible to make a full-time career out of racing. Job security wasn't guaranteed. If a driver did not win, he was replaced. Ned didn't want that happening to his boys.

In high school, Dale was an all-conference selection in football, basketball, baseball, and golf. He was named 1975 Athlete of the Year when a senior at the Newton-Conover High School, and in 1974 and 1975, he was the North Carolina High School Southern District Seven Golfer of the Year.

Glenn excelled in baseball and golf as well. Following high school, Glenn went on to the University of North Carolina and then worked at the family's lumber business.

Dale didn't talk very much about racing, said Ned, until he drove in his first race. He got his start in a way that mirrors Ned's entry into the sport. Dale and some friends built a car. The weekend they were to race, the mother of the friend who was to drive died. Dale took over the wheel. "After that first race he was hooked," Ned said.

In 1976, Dale won a Late Model Sportsman event at Hickory in which he passed Dale Earnhardt with four laps remaining in the race.

A year later, when he was 20, Dale, along with a group of friends, formed a team to run at Hickory. "He and a couple of buddies got in-

Dale Jarrett leads the field to the green flag for the start of a race at the Charlotte Motor Speedway.

volved," Ned said. "I didn't know about it for a time. When they got the car built they needed an engine. Dale came to me and said, 'I think I can get to drive the car if I can get an engine.'"

Ned pointed his son toward some folks who could get an engine for the car, and Dale's racing career was off and running.

Following his father's tracks into the sport, Dale, in 1977, debuted in the Limited Sportsman division at the Hickory Motor Speedway and won the track's Rookie of the Year title for the division. Except for the pavement, it was the same track where Ned had made his debut in 1953.

"I watched the early part of the race, and I thought, 'you know, he's got some potential,'" Ned said on seeing his son race for the first time.

"I always thought it was something I wanted to do, but I was 20 years old before I had the opportunity to get in a stock car," Dale told fans in an on-line chat session in 1997. "I had raced go-karts before, but most of my time was spent in other sports. Mostly on the golf course. But since I got in that car at Hickory, I knew that was going to be my focus for the next 20 years."

Despite their efforts to steer him in another direction, Ned and Martha Jarrett had a son in racing. "It was not that I didn't want him in racing," Ned said. "But he seemed destined for a professional sports career. A lot of people felt he had the potential of making it as a pro golfer. He had scholarship offers. I knew how tough it was in racing," he said. "I knew the sacrifices he would have to make in racing if he ever were to get to the top. I didn't want him to go through that."

Dale once said of his brother: "Glenn, I guess played a really big hand in me getting started and getting the opportunity," Dale said. "He started racing when my Dad owned Hickory Speedway, and gave me the opportunity to get around race cars, and be a part of it, and learn something about them. It was fun to race with Glenn. Glenn was a good race driver."

Around the same time, Ned was planning for his own future. The same year that Dale made his debut at Hickory, Ned sold his interest in the track and focused on a full-time broadcasting career.

The year he retired, Jarrett did two radio broadcasts of local races. He had also done a few other radio telecasts during the '60s and '70s. His first attempt at television occurred in 1969 when he worked on a closed-circuit telecast of the Daytona 500.

In 1977, auto racing was rarely televised. No Winston Cup races were carried live in their entirety, although bits and pieces were offered during ABC's "Wide World of Sports." Still, fan loyalty for the sport was growing. "I personally made the decision to build another career in racing," Ned recalled. "I'd been building a broadcast business. It was not yet a living. But I decided that this sport was heading in that direction. I believed I could build up a program for myself and make a living doing that."

A year later, Ned made his debut as part of the Motor Racing Network's live radio broadcasts of NASCAR racing. That got his foot in the door. Two years later, when CBS decided to air the Daytona live from start to finish, they called on Jarrett to offer expert analysis.

He has been part of the telecast ever since. "Your first broadcast is similar to your early days of racing," Jarrett told a reporter, "when you have butterflies in your stomach and don't know exactly how things are going to go or what you're going to say."

Within a few years, two of the Jarretts were in racing and looking toward the future.

6

DIFFERENT CAREERS

The racing careers of Dale and Glenn Jarrett started off on similar paths, but differed widely later on.

After racing at Hickory, Dale landed a full-time driving job in 1982 on the newly formed Busch Grand National tour. It's not quite Winston Cup, but close.

In his first year, Dale started 29 events on the series, which uses cars similar to those in Winston Cup and runs on many of the same tracks. He earned one top-five finish and 15 top-10 finishes. All totaled, he won $27,261 in prize money.

He won his first race on the series in 1986 at the .375-mile long Orange County Speedway in Rougemont, North Carolina. He started on the pole and averaged 95.487 mph to win. He entered the series driving for Horace Isenhower, and has driven for him on the Busch level ever since.

Dale Jarrett sits while his pit crew works on his race car during a pit stop at the running of the Pennsylvania 500 NASCAR race in July 1997.

Isenhower provided Dale with with a luxury Glenn didn't have: cars and financial backing. Dale didn't have to worry about sinking his own money into the team, whereas Glenn, without the benefit of driving for someone else, had to fund his own operation. Starting in 1984, Glenn became a regular on the Busch series, although he stepped down in 1988. "It became a necessity," he said. "I was funding the thing out of my pocket."

At the time, Glenn was an unmarried sales representative for a Louisville, Kentucky, company. Not having to worry about supporting a family allowed him to pursue racing, although it eventually became a drain on him.

He struggled with poorly performing equipment, which ultimately brought down his own on-track performance. He entered a few Winston Cup races, but was winless in both series.

Away from the track, he and his father launched a Honda car dealership that demanded his time. Eventually, racing was sacrificed for business. "I had been running this deal on my own," he said. "The equipment was old and banged up. It was with all those thoughts that I decided to leave. I've regretted it ever since."

At that point the brothers' racing careers headed in different directions. Dale continued to drive while Glenn branched off into the business world. "The biggest difference between Glenn and Dale was that Glenn never really got any top-notch equipment," Ned said.

Dale agreed. "I believe that Glenn just never got the right opportunity which is what it's all about: getting in the right situation."

While racing on the Busch series, Dale was looking ahead. Two years after his debut in the Busch ranks, he made his first Winston Cup start on April 29, 1984, at Martinsville Speedway. He started the race in the 24th spot and finished 14th. He made two more starts that year. In 1986 he raced in one event, which he failed to finish.

In 1987, Dale landed a full-time Winston Cup ride with car owner Eric Freedlander. He ran 24 races that season, finishing twice in the top 10. He also started 27 Busch races in 1987 and won one.

In 1988, Dale's Busch racing took a back seat to the Winston Cup series. It was not an easy ride by any stretch of the imagination. He drove for three different owners in early 1988 before landing a regular job with Cale Yarborough, a legendary racer who was slowly retiring from driving. He ran 19 races for Yarborough that year and got one top 10 finish.

In 1989, Yarborough cut Jarrett midway through the season. Dale returned to the Busch series, but struggled financially, coming near the brink of bankruptcy. He lived in his grandfather's garage apartment. "He was chasing a dream," Glenn once said.

In 1990, after Neil Bonnett was injured at Charlotte, the famed Wood Brothers racing team hired Jarrett to fill in for the recuperating Bonnett. He entered the deal knowing full well that if Bonnett came back, he was out of a job. But he worked hard and remained with the team the following year.

Midway through the 1991 season—his second with the Wood Brothers—Dale signed a deal to drive for former Washington Redskins coach Joe Gibbs for the 1992 season. He still had to finish out the season with the Wood Brothers, however.

He entered the 1992 Champion 400 race at the Michigan International Speedway as a lame duck driver for the Wood Brothers team. But that didn't show in his driving style. He qualified his Citgo Ford in the 11th starting position. By lap 188, Jarrett was in fourth position when a crash brought out a caution flag. Like his competitors, Jarrett dove into the pits. While others took on gas and tires, Jarrett's team opted for gas only. He exited pit road in first place.

Davey Allison, fourth at the restart, blazed past Mark Martin's Ford and into second

This photo taken by a race car camera shows Jeff Green (3) and Greg Sacks (33) locked up at turn three during the Miami 300 at Homestead Motorsports Complex in November 1995. Dale Jarrett won the race.

place, which set up a side-by-side battle with Jarrett for the final two laps of the 200-lap race. Ned Jarrett, who was working the race as part of ESPN's broadcast team, was silent.

Going into the final lap, Allison's car was a nose ahead of Jarrett's. Their cars touched, sending a plume of tire smoke into the air. Jarrett held on to win by about the length of a football. "I just hope it was as good for everybody else as it was for us," Jarrett said after the race. "You just sit around and imagine these things."

In the broadcast booth, Ned was a professional. "I don't know what I did," he said later. "I'm sure I hollered, because I was so excited. With five laps to go I really got nervous, but I still did my part on TV."

Once the broadcast was over he immediately dropped his headset and headed for Victory Lane to celebrate with his son.

"We rubbed a couple of times there, and I hope [Allison] thought it was what he would call clean racing." Dale said. "I wasn't trying to wreck anybody. I could have gone into [turn] three and probably run him all the way to the wall. But I think I gave him just enough room to race."

The win was the first for Dale in 129 Winston Cup starts.

As Dale was winning his first Winston Cup start, his brother Glenn was making his return to the sport.

After a few years of self-imposed exile from racing, Glenn got an offer from Sports Channel America to provide color commentary for eight Busch Grand National races. It took some arm twisting, but Glenn eventually was coaxed into the job. He debuted in 1990 as color analyst at a race held at Lanier Raceway in Gainsville, Georgia. "I knew it was time," he said. "I can still remember the feeling, I still have to catch my voice when talking about it. When I walked back into the garage, there they all were, my friends, the guys I used to race against. I honestly felt I'd come home. This is what I was meant to do. These are the people I like being around."

Glenn turned that eight-race opportunity into a full-blown broadcasting career. He went on to work for TBS, Jefferson Pilot Productions, and as a radio color analyst alongside Ken Squier.

In the early '90s, as Dale was winning his first race, Glenn joined the Nashville Network, which was starting to broadcast racing events.

In 1995, after three seasons driving for Joe Gibbs, Dale announced he would be moving on. He had won two races with Gibbs, including the Daytona 500, and finished high in many others. But he was lured away by Robert Yates, who needed a driver to replace Ernie Irvan in the Texaco/Havoline Ford. Irvan was seriously injured in a 1994 wreck at Michigan, and it was unclear when and if he would ever return to driving. Once again, Jarrett took the job, knowing there was a chance that if Irvan returned, he would be without a ride.

He won one race for Yates in 1995 and earned $1,363,158. It was a difficult season, however. Irvan had been a strong competitor in the car, and Jarrett and the team struggled. That led naysayers to say Jarrett wasn't as good as Irvan. "Even though things might not have been going the way I wanted them to go, I came to realize that there was a reason for all of this," he said then. "You have to understand that even though we weren't winning races and running up front all the time, I was still doing exactly what I wanted to be doing, and that was driving a race car with a very good group of people, so there wasn't as much to be down about as people perceived."

Irvan returned later that year, putting Jarrett's 1996 season in doubt. After contemplating going out on his own, Jarrett and Yates struck a deal to form a second team. With backing from Ford, the new team debuted at the 1996 Daytona 500, and Dale won.

Dale went on to win three other races, and as the season's end neared, he was in a tight points battle for the series championship. To win the title in the final event at Atlanta, he needed points leader Terry Labonte and second-place Jeff Gordon to fall out of the race early. Jarrett would need to lead almost every lap to win the race. Dale knew going in that his chances of winning the title were small.

"There's still a chance for us," Jarrett said before the event. "But it's a slim, slim chance, especially because we're trying to overtake two people instead of just one. Both have to have trouble at Atlanta, and we'd have to have a perfect race."

Jarrett's shot at the title in 1996 ended unsuccessfully, but he would return.

7

THE LEGEND
GOES ON

Dale Jarrett entered the 1997 season brimming with confidence.

Having come off a third-place finish in the Winston Cup points standings in 1996, Jarrett and his Ford Quality Care–sponsored team had momentum on their side.

He won four races in 1996, doubling his career total for the previous 11 years of racing in NASCAR's premiere level. And he had overcome the 1995 outing, which was tough on the team.

Jarrett and his crew chief Todd Parrott, son of legendary crew chief Buddy Parrott, had gelled as a team and were of like minds when it came to strategy on the track.

Dale finished 23rd in the season-opening Daytona 500, and by the third race of the season he had fought back to be third overall in

Dale Jarrett gets a kiss from his mother, Martha, as his father, Ned, looks on in Victory Lane after Dale won the UAW-GM Quality 500 at the Charlotte Motor Speedway on October 5, 1997.

the points race. Then he won the fourth race of the year at Atlanta to take the points lead.

"[After the first three races] dad just kept telling me to keep doing the things we were doing," he said after the win. "We were running great, things just weren't going our way, and we just had to keep doing what we were doing, and that we would get to Victory Lane." Jarrett said his father had been his biggest supporter and that it was great to have a friend who understood the business.

Dale was already talking about winning the championship, which was months away. "You start thinking about a championship at Daytona," he said. "We learned that [in 1996]. You have to race every race with that championship in mind. I think that we have the team and the people that it takes to win a championship."

Jarrett, whose Winston Cup career got off to a shaky start, was now a contender. Over a period of a dozen years, he had risen to the top of NASCAR's ranks, a position held by his father three decades earlier.

Winning at Atlanta gave Dale a boost. Winning early in the season is important, he said. "If you can win early, you don't put as much pressure on yourself and they seem to come easier, because you're just doing the things you've been doing, instead of pressing and trying to make things happen," he said.

The win was also gratifying because it was the first track on the circuit where both Ned and Dale had won a race. Ned picked up a win at Atlanta in 1964, and now Dale had etched his name into the record books.

Dale followed up his win at Atlanta with a win at Darlington and a second-place finish at the newly opened Texas Motor Speedway. He maintained his points lead until Talladega in May, when a 32nd-place finish dropped him to third overall. As in the past, Dale was tough most of the season, holding onto fourth in the points for several weeks until a series of top finishes near the end put him in third and then second with two races to go.

He went into the next to last race of the year at Phoenix in second behind 1995 champion Jeff Gordon.

Jarrett & Co. gambled and brought a new car to Phoenix. It hadn't been raced in 1997, and it was a new design that was supposed to be better on flat tracks. The car had run in 1996, although it was rebuilt for the Phoenix event.

Jeff Gordon (24) rams into the back of then–race leader Dale Jarrett (88) in the Miller 500 at Dover Downs International Speedway in Dover, Delaware. Gordon broke his radiator in the mishap, and Jarrett blew his engine later. Neither finished the race.

Nevertheless, Jarrett was going into a race on a track where his rival Jeff Gordon had fared well. "We're not concerned," he said. "We have to do what we can do. We can't control what they do at all. Even though you may have a good record somewhere, that doesn't always work out. You don't know what is going to happen. A flat tire can change everything. An accident certainly changes a lot of things. You just don't know what is going to happen, so we have to concern ourselves with our car and making it the best it can be."

Jarrett qualified ninth at Phoenix and won the race, which combined with Gordon's 17th place finish left him in second, 77 points behind, with one race to go.

For the second consecutive year Jarrett went into the season-ending race in Atlanta with a shot at the title. Following Phoenix, he and the team had two weeks to prepare for the event. "I think myself and my team are glad to have a little bit of time," he said. "We do have a lot of momentum going and a lot of confidence in our race team, But we want to make sure we're completely ready for Atlanta."

Jarrett said it was great to be able to talk about being in the championship hunt with a race to go. He was confident, too, because Gordon had the title to lose, while he could go into the race and risk everything for the win. "It is definitely more difficult to protect a lead than it is to try to come from behind," he said. "I'm sure there is some tension [in Gordon's team]."

Asked why he was always so positive, Jarrett said it was important for a driver to show confidence and to have confidence in his team. "I can remember watching my dad," he said. "I remember how he handled it and what he was going through. It can be a very difficult situation if you let it be. I think what we try to do is make it a very positive experience. And that's something I did gain from my dad."

Jarrett qualified his Ford Quality Care–sponsored car in the third starting position. Gordon, who wrecked his primary car in practice, started 37th. Gordon only had to finish 18th or better to win his second title.

Jarrett didn't let the adversity get to him, however. He raced hard and finished second.

Dale Jarrett (88), driving a Ford, passes Geoff Bodine in the closing laps of the Dura-Lube 500 Winston Cup NASCAR Race at Phoenix International Speedway. Jarrett won the race.

Gordon, three laps off the leader, finished 17th and won the title. Jarrett was just 14 points shy of the title. "We had a tremendous season," he said. "Certainly we wanted to win the championship, but we realized we gave it everything we possibly could, and just came up a little bit short. But as far as we were con-

Dale Jarrett of Hickory, North Carolina, holds his trophy in Victory Lane after winning the TranSouth Financial 400 at Darlington Raceway in South Carolina, March 22, 1998.

cerned, as a race team, we were extremely excited about what we were able to do. We led
more laps, and finished more laps and miles
than anybody else out there so that says a lot
about your team. We won seven races, second
only to the guy who won the championship."

And while Dale was climbing NASCAR's
ladder, the sport was growing, too. NASCAR
has undergone unprecedented growth, especially during the 1990s. Attendance levels
have climbed to record highs, topping six
million people in 1997. And television rat-
ings have soared.

And as one of the families that stayed with
the sport through several generations, the
Jarretts are a part of NASCAR's foundation.
Dale, Glenn, and Ned have served as ambas-
sadors for the sport over the years and helped
improve the overall perception of racing to
many who come into contact with the sport for
the first time.

Dale alone makes upward of 100 off-track
appearances for the sponsors of his Winston
Cup and Busch teams each year, while Glenn
and Ned push the sport during race telecasts
and in personal speaking engagements.

When Ned retired in 1966, NASCAR was
staging nearly 60 races a year under its Grand
National banner. Three decades later, the
schedule hovers around 33 events a season on
the Winston Cup circuit, with plans for gradual expansion.

Although the 1997 title eluded Jarrett, the
year marked another important milestone for
NASCAR and the Jarretts.

On March 29, 1997, 44 years after Ned
Jarrett made his debut at Hickory Motor

Dale Jarrett tries to entertain his one-year-old son, Zachary, in Victory Lane after he won the Busch Clash at Daytona International Speedway in Florida on February 11, 1996. Another potential race car driver?

Speedway, Jason Jarrett, Dale's son born in 1975, made his Busch Grand National debut at Hickory. Qualifying trials for the race were rained out, so Jason's starting position was dictated by car owners' points. He started 28th in the 31-car field and finished 21st, four laps off the lead. He earned $3,045 for the day's work. He started two other races in

1997 with an eye toward increasing the total in the future. Plans were to have Dale and Jason split the Busch series schedule in 1998.

"Jason, I'm excited about what he has in front of him here," Dale said. "We're excited for him. He's learned an awful lot about racing and race cars in a short period of time. I think that he realizes the chance that he has, and what were doing now at DAJ Racing is trying to give him equipment that is up to his potential."

Unlike Dale and Glenn, who were young kids when Ned retired, Jason grew up with his dad a top competitor in the sport. According to Ned, it should come as no surprise that Jason is pursuing a racing career. "Certainly, we had to expect that he would be interested," Ned said. "For most of his life, Dale has been racing. Dale was only 9 when I quit racing and Glenn was only 15. They were not around, although we would take them to races, not as much as Jason was with his dad."

"Jason didn't show an inkling toward racing until after high school," said Ned. "But once he did, he was totally engulfed with it."

Ned Jarrett finds a great deal of satisfaction in having a son battling for a championship, another son working in broadcasting, a daughter married to a top crew chief, and now a grandson racing.

"It's a great feeling," he said. "I guess I'm living part of what I gave up when I quit driving through [Dale]. I have an equal feeling with Glenn and his broadcasting. I have two sons following my footsteps as a driver and the other as a broadcaster. To be able to live through them, with things I might have missed, has been wonderful."

CHRONOLOGY

1932 Ned Miller Jarrett is born on October 12 in Newton, North Carolina

1950 Glenn Jarrett is born on August 11

1953 Ned Jarrett enters his first NASCAR Grand National Race on August 29 at Hickory Motor Speedway

1956 Dale Arnold Jarrett born on November 26

1957 Ned Jarrett wins first of two consecutive NASCAR National Sportsman Championships

1959 Ned Jarrett increases his schedule on NASCAR Grand National Series

1961 Ned Jarrett wins first of two NASCAR Grand National Championships

1965 Ned Jarrett wins second NASCAR Grand National title and vows to retire; wins famed Southern 500 at Darlington Speedway

1966 Ned Jarrett retires from racing with 50 wins

1975 Jason Jarrett born on October 14

1976 Glenn Jarrett makes his racing debut at Hickory Motor Speedway

1979 Ned Jarrett appears on CBS live flag-to-flag telecast of the Daytona 500, the first Winston Cup Race ever to air live in its entirety on television

1982 Dale Jarrett races full time on NASCAR Busch Grand National Series

1984 Glenn Jarrett debuts on Busch Series; Dale makes first Winston Cup start

1986 Dale Jarrett wins first Busch race

1987 Dale Jarrett moves into Winston Cup racing full time

1988 Glenn Jarrett retires from racing

1991 Dale Jarrett beats Davey Allison by eight inches to win his first Winston Cup race in the Champion 400 at Michigan International Speedway (now simply called Michigan Speedway)

1993 Dale Jarrett wins Daytona 500; he repeats the feat in 1996

1997 Jason Jarrett makes his Busch Series debut on March 29 at the Hickory Motor Speedway and finishes 21st

1997 Dale Jarrett finishes second in Winston Cup points race

1999 Dale Jarrett wins his first Winston Cup championship

2000 Dale Jarrett wins Winston Cup Series; Jason Jarrett takes 4th place in ACRA series

2001 Jason becomes a full time racer in the ACRA series and competes for Rookie of the Year

STATISTICS

Ned Jarrett (Winston Cup Series)

Year	Races	Wins	Finishes 2-5	Finishes 6-11	Money Won
1953	2	0	0	0	$125
1954	2	0	0	0	25
1955	3	0	0	0	260
1956	2	0	0	0	60
1957	1	0	0	0	50
1958	0	0	0	0	0
1959	17	2	2	3	3,860
1960	40	5	15	6	25,438
1961	46	1	22	11	41,056
1962	52	6	13	16	43,444
1963	53	8	24	7	45,844
1964	59	15	25	5	71,925
1965	54	13	29	3	93,625
1966	21	0	5	3	23,255
Totals	352	50	135	54	348,967

Glenn Jarrett (Winston Cup Series)

Year	Races	Wins	Finishes 2-5	Finishes 6-11	Money Won
1978	1	0	0	0	$2,940
1979	2	0	0	0	2,745
1980	2	0	0	0	4,435
1981	3	0	0	0	12,650
1982	1	0	0	0	735
1983	1	0	0	0	1,200
1985	0	0	0	0	4,200
Totals	10	0	0	0	28,905

STATISTICS

Dale Jarrett (Winston Cup Series)

YEAR	RACES	WINS	FINISHES 2-5	FINISHES 6-11	MONEY WON
1984	3	0	0	0	$7,305
1986	1	0	0	0	990
1987	24	0	0	2	143,405
1988	29	0	0	1	118,640
1989	29	0	2	3	232,317
1990	24	0	1	6	214,495
1991	29	1	2	5	444,256
1992	29	0	2	6	418,648
1993	30	1	12	5	1,242,394
1994	30	1	3	5	893,754
1995	31	1	8	5	1,363,158
1996	31	4	13	4	2,985,418
1997	32	7	11	5	3,240,362
1998	33	3	19	5	2,346,535
1999	34	4	20	5	3,590,829
2000	38	4	11	9	5,225,499
2001	36	4	12	6	4,437,644
TOTALS	463	30	116	72	$26,905,649

Jason Jarrett (Busch Series)

YEAR	RACES	WINS	FINISHES 2-5	FINISHES 6-11	MONEY WON
1997	3	0	0	0	$10,695
1999	8	0	0	0	130,735
2000	40	0	0	0	287,115
TOTALS	51	0	0	0	$428,545

FURTHER READING

Center, Bill. *NASCAR: The Thunder of America.* New York: Harper Collins, 1998.

Chapin, Kim. *Fast As White Lightning.* New York: The Dial Press, 1981.

Golenbock, Peter, and Greg Fielden. *The Stock Car Racing Encyclopedia.* Indianapolis, Indiana: Macmillan, 1997.

Huff, Richard. *Behind the Wall: A Season on the NASCAR Circuit.* Chicago: Bonus Books, 1992.

Huff, Richard. *The Insider's Guide to Stock Car Racing.* Chicago: Bonus Books, 1997.

Pearce, Al, and Bill Fleischman. *Inside Sports Magazine NASCAR Racing: The Ultimate Fan Guide.* Detroit, Michigan: Visible Ink, 1998.

ABOUT THE AUTHOR

Richard Huff is an award-winning journalist and author. His previous books include *Behind the Wall, A Season on the NASCAR Circuit, The Insider's Guide to Stock Car Racing,* and *Formula One Racing.* He is a staff writer and motor sports columnist for the New York *Daily News.* His work has appeared in such national publications as *NASCAR Magazine, Inside NASCAR, Stock Car Racing Magazine, Video Review, The Washington Journalism Review, Seventeen,* and *Hot Rod, Jr.* He lives in Highland, New Jersey, with his wife, Michelle, and son, Ryan.

ACKNOWLEDGEMENTS

The author would like to thank the following people, without whose help the creation of this book would have been impossible: Ned Jarrett, Charlie Munch, Michelle and Ryan Huff, Mom, and Cathe Slocum.

INDEX